NOW

NOW

BY

KHALID EL BEY

DEYEL PUBLISHING COMPANY

217 WEST KENNEDY STREET,

SYRACUSE, NEW YORK [13205]

CREATIVE RESEARCH SOCIETY

SYRACUSE, NEW YORK

Printed 2012

For information: www.khalidelbey.com

Cover illustration by Khalid El Bey

Published by
DEYEL PUBLISHING
217 West Kennedy Street, Syracuse, New York [13205]

CREATIVE RESEARCH SOCIETY
Syracuse New York

Printed in the United States of America.

DEDICATION

I would like to dedicate this book to EVERYONE, with the sincere hope that it will be of some help in your efforts to gain control over your lives.

I would also like to dedicate this book to my children for being my inspiration and creating in me the aspiration to make their life experiences and the life experiences of others easier.

- *Khalid El Bey*

CONTENTS

Chapter

Page

Preface	*7*
Introduction	*13*
1. Polarity	18
2. Shadow Time	42
3. Time Travel	56
4. There Is No Tomorrow	68
5. Now	84
About the Author	96

PREFACE

An old Buddhist teaching states "the meeting of Heaven (time) and Earth (space) gives birth to the realm of illusion."

The interface of polar opposites, simply put, gives rise to what we perceive as manifest reality. Humanity's self-realization/self-awareness developed as a result of the need for the True Self to gather and process incoming information from the outside world, and this gave rise to the ego, whose true purpose is to interface with the outside world and bring that experience to the attention of the True Self.

Khalid Bey's work demonstrates the true source of human suffering: the fact that we have reversed the roles of the True Self and the ego. We have "fallen asleep" and allowed the ego to run the show, to the point that we now erroneously believe we ARE the ego, hence we are our experiences. We begin to then live within the artificial constructs of "past" and "future;" of fatalism and uncertainty, wherein we take on the characteristics of these realms, believing our circumstances are either forever fixed or hopelessly nebulous. Either condition renders the sufferer inconstant and paralyzed, unable to change their conditions.

Between Heaven (time) and Earth (space) is a third midpoint dimension; Man (Energy/Will). An old Moorish proverb states "there is no Good that does not come with its admixture of evil, yet God always provides us with the means of throwing off the evil from the Good." We have become so comfortable in the hells of Past and Future and the limited liability of allowing the ego to lead our existence, that the mere idea of leaving either Past or Future and coming to the real world where the True Self resides is literally a notion that we directly relate to physical death, and in a very real sense this is not far from the truth.

The alchemical admonition "solve et coagula" teaches us that the fixed state of the ego must be made malleable, and this is a kind of death, and is affected by using the Will/Energy to direct the projection of the ego inwards towards the True Self; away from Past and Future towards the NOW.

"NOW" is an unfamiliar, terrifying, yet exciting place to be. Khalid Bey challenges the reader to "go where no man (the reader) has gone before." "NOW" compels you to die; to murder (sublimate) the ego and destroy the comfortable prisons it has constructed, abandon illusion, and explore the real world. Be certain that if you follow Mr. Bey's course of action YOU WILL DIE; but in reality the fear of death is really the fear of the meeting with the True Self.

- *Sharif Anael Bey*

INTRODUCTION

This very moment where you are right now is the most important moment in your life. It holds the solution or the key to all of your problems and/or concerns. There is not a more opportune moment in time for you to lay a foundation towards a more productive, purposeful and fulfilling life.

There are many of us who suffer silently day in and day out. Dissatisfaction with the decisions and/or actions of our past and fear of the uncertainty of tomorrow increases our stress levels to the point of high blood pressure, cardiac arrest, aneurysms, strokes, etc. Every single person on this planet wants and deserves a peaceful and productive existence. We search high and low for opportunity, hoping to find an answer or a solution somewhere out there in the world, but often with very little to no success. Such a dilemma creates in the average person confusion resulting in intellectual and emotional handicaps so severe, that the persons in question self-destruct, sometimes purposefully.

Our lack of understanding about life, our preoccupation with the superficial, our inability remain consistently attentive allows for our lives to spin hopelessly out of control leading to repeat dissatisfaction and despair. In more than half of the cases alcoholism and drug abuse becomes the escape.

This work is intended to be used as a guide for repairing one's life; to provide the reader the tools necessary for the reconstruction of their thinking. My suggestion is that you read this book more than once, and refer to this book in times of confusion. In each chapter I attempt to provide proof to the reader of certain ideas or principles that may assist them in their efforts towards self-improvement. To empower an individual to be self efficient is one of the greatest gifts you could give, leading them to a feeling of

freedom never before experienced.

- *KEB*

Part One

POLARITY

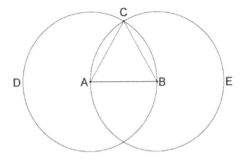

The first problem of Euclid suggests that for everything that exists there is an opposite. For example, up and down, left and right, inside and outside, male and female, darkness and light, truth and falsehood, God and the Devil, powerful and weak, wide and narrow, fast and slow, etc.; every force in existence has an opposite or receiver of said force.

When one thinks of opposites what naturally comes to mind is the idea of two separate things; but even within a single object, opposing natures or polarity can be found. One example to consider is this: when a child is born he receives a total of 46 chromosomes: 23 come from the father and 23 come from his opposite (the mother). Another example to consider is the fact that a human being possesses a mind, the opposite of which could be said to be a physical body.

A house or similar structure clearly displays polarity having an interior and exterior. Within our bodies are red blood cells that have the primary function of supplying oxygen to all body tissue and organs, and (opposite in its character to oxygen) carbon dioxide is the waste that is the result of the body's metabolism, which eventually exits the body. White blood cells help combat infection(s). Some white blood cells act as scavengers by engulfing foreign particles (such as bacteria) and destroying them. In each example, opposing natures or behaviors are displayed: red blood cells, which expresses a creative behavior versus white blood cells, which demonstrates a destructive behavior; also oxygen which enters versus carbon dioxide, which exits.

When considering the idea of polarity what must be realized is that for every idea or object, there is an opposing idea or object providing the former balance. Within the universe there exists what should be the most obvious, but is probably the most unobvious polarity: space or an apparent nothingness, and the objects which occupy said space or nothingness. Consider this: the planet Jupiter due to its size and magnetic power acts as an anchor to the Sun. There exists a tug-of-war between the Sun and Jupiter that keeps the planets between them in order. In other words, the gravitational pull between the two larger planetary bodies, each at opposite ends in this example help the smaller planetary bodies maintain a relatively consistent, balanced orbit. Our Sun according to science is reportedly the tail end of an explosion initiated at some other point in space billions of miles away. In biblical lore, polarity is displayed by the changing of the names of Abram to Abraham and Jacob to Israel. Abram to Abraham being the spirit incarnating, while Jacob to Israel being its ascension from the gross (matter) to the most pure (spirit).

If we were to take a look at two of the three supernal elements, fire and water (air being the third), one would not only notice that each is the opposite of the other, but also that within each of these two elements there exist the potential for creation and destruction. The initial Life impulse with its very first movement creates a 'pocket of air or archetypal container', which is clearly the resulting opposite (effect) of its movement.

Polarity is defined as: [*Physics*] – *1a. the property or characteristic that produces unequal physical effects at different points in a body or system, as (with) a magnate or storage battery.* (Dictionary.com) Translation: the physical characteristics (or appearance) or "make-up" or "behavior" of a thing or idea, which establishes exact differences or effects, from the object or idea to which it is being compared. (I'm not sure if that translation was any simpler.)

An understanding of polarity or opposing forces is the <u>beginning</u> of the understanding of all of creation. If we use for example a fairly recognizable or simple situation, such as a desire to eat caused superficially by stomach growling and hunger pains, one could recognize cause and effect. This same principle applies to every part of existence, for there is (almost) no effect without cause. Every human emotion has an opposing emotion which works to offset the former. This of course is a very important factor for one who attempts the sometimes impossible discipline of smiling in the face of adversity. In chemistry every element has an opposing element, just as in mundane (physical) life there is the ever appearance of polarity: opposing political parties; the sky and the earth; movable and immovable objects, etc. Take a moment to observe all around and witness the existence of opposites everywhere and in everything.

Molecular Polarity

An Explanation

While reading this section, do you best to remain attentive, and stay with me; if you haven't already, you will catch on. Polarity is a physical property (or appearance of difference[s]) of or between compounds, objects, etc., which relates other physical properties such as melting and boiling points, solubility, and intermolecular interactions between molecules. The properties mentioned, i.e. melting points, solubility, intermolecular interactions, simply imply a change or transformation happening to the object(s) in question. An example would be ice, which is solid in characteristic, melting or changing to liquid once place in a warmer climate. Relationship (comparison/correspondence) is therefore established between the solid ice and the climate, and between the ice and water.

For the most part, there is a direct relation between the polarity of a molecule and number and types of polar or non-polar (referred to as "covalent") bonds which are present. Covalent (or non-polar) bonding is when two atoms share two electrons. The two electrons shared by the atoms are attracted to the nucleus of both atoms. Neither atom completely loses or gains electrons as in ionic bonding. In Non-polar bonds there is <u>an equal sharing</u> of electrons; balance therefore is the result. Polar bonding is when there is an <u>unequal</u> sharing of electrons, causing a domination of one (extreme) 'force' or in this case, the domination of one electron over the other. If one were to have a scale and on one side placed one stone and on the other side placed two stones of equal size and mass to the first (stone), an understanding of Polar bonding would be received. In a simpler explanation: Polar bonding is when too much energy is given in one direction or to one extreme, thereby causing the neglect of the opposite extreme and creating an imbalance. Another example: If the Sun's gravitational pull increased to the point where it overpowered Jupiter, the smaller planets in between would move out of orbit, eventually crashing and burning on the Sun. Non-polar bonding is when there is an equal distribution of energy in both directions; **neither extreme is overpowered nor neglected and so balance is maintained**. This means that the balance or imbalance is determined by the number of Non-polar bonds there are in a body or system in comparison to the number of Polar bonds in that same body or system. Put simply, balance and equilibrium in ones circumstances (or the lack thereof) is determined by the number of non-polar situations there are, compared to the number of polar situations there are in said circumstances.

In life most of us are obligated by circumstance(s) to find work or a career to enable us to take care of ourselves, our families and other responsibilities. As commonly found in most situations, a majority of the energy that one has tends to be focused in <u>one</u> of the two directions. This 'polar bonding' causes an imbalance, resulting in stress, worry, dissatisfaction, disruption and failure in the opposite area that is receiving less energy.

In politics and government too much of a (monetary) focus on the war in Iraq and Afghanistan, and / or the outsourcing of jobs to compete in the global economy had caused a recession here in the United States. Where the mind is concerned, too much energy or focus on negatives, such as fear of failure and disappointment, causes one to neglect and therefore "paralyze" the opposite emotional responses of courage and satisfaction.

Conclusion

One would wonder about the <u>reason</u> or purpose for an opposing force; an idea that has been known and spoken about by many more qualified than I on the subject. The idea of polarity existing in all things or in all of Life creates for many the most confusing and contradicting ideas and circumstances. This very 'necessary' contradiction though, is the mechanism needed (and used, knowingly and / or unknowingly) to validate Life. This reality is displayed by the explanation of ratio and proportion in Mathematics, or by the manifestation of 'bad' in the midst of 'good'. One way to display the 'need' or value for contradiction is to ask yourself "how would one know good, were it not for bad". "How could one accurately categorize the idea of a Devil, were there not an idea of a 'God' to compare him or her to?"

Every physical thing that exists is identified and categorized by its physical characteristics *being compared* to another object's physical characteristics. I must though repeat one fact, so to forever embed it into the reader's memory: All objects (or ideas) which appear separate from other objects (or ideas) are in fact 'whole' themselves and therefore dual in nature. Birth and death though appearing to be contradicting or separate events are in fact the same phenomenon, Life. It is a repeated entrance into and exit out of a 'looping' or continuum; and it is this 'continuum' or world of events, definition and finality into which Life chaotically leaps for no other apparent purpose, except to validate its own existence. Through polarity, the universe and all that exist within it and without it is noticed, contradicted, established and/or validated; for absent such contradictions leading to validation, Life and all that is the result of Life would be naught.

Part Two

SHADOW TIME

The idea of home has become, for me, a very interesting concept. When one contemplates home what immediately comes to mind is the house or apartment within which one resides. In addition to the aforementioned, when considering the concept of home one also thinks of a place to which one would always return; a place where comfort and security could be found; where one's family and / or loved ones dwell.

For many, the idea of home at times is broader in context. "Home" could refer to a town, city, state, or even one's native country. There are even some cases where the concept of home might not apply to any of the above mentioned locales, but instead simply refers to specific surroundings, i.e. persons or a familiar environment. When examined further, the idea of home becomes less tangible; and more abstract. The idea of home suggests for most people, stability. Yet the general idea of home (stability) falls short when a person relocates or changes her residence. In many cases most people do not remain in the same house, apartment, or even the exact same area (code) of their birth; so it may be argued that a person throughout the course of her life has many homes; unless it could be better argued that home might imply something altogether totally different.

Think about this for a moment; imagine what it would be like if your entire memory failed. If an individual's memory failed completely, he would not recognize his own thumb let alone his house or neighborhood. It could be argued that all we are or all that we claim to be is recorded or programmed into our memory. Our ideas of comfort and security; our ability to recognize our house, neighborhood, even our family, depends 'totally' on the 'compartment' of mind that houses the memory. Is it possible that what one identifies as home is in fact a memory of a specific feeling (comfort, security, etc.)? Clearly one's true home, if such an idea could be coined, is not necessarily characterized by the physical structure that one dwells in for any particular amount of time; for it appears that this "sense of home" could be established where ever one chooses to dwell.

I would argue that no matter one's surroundings; no matter the number of people living with an individual within the same structure (house); no matter the number of physical structures (houses) one has occupied; said individual(s) lives alone in his/her own home/world (mind). A person's external behavior is a reflection of his thoughts. How one communicates, dresses, or acts in general is the result of the "mind stuff" that he experiences <u>all unto himself</u>. Despite what might be assumed regarding the everyday life of any particular person, no person has ever had any "physical" visitors; nor will he ever have such visitors in his <u>true home</u>, or his true place of comfort and security (his head/mind).

Each and every one of us resides in a place that is peopled by ghost. What I mean by this is that all that we are and all that we know is the result of our memories; those intangible, fluffy, less than crystallized images housed in the shadows. This is the place where each person on this planet resides. It is here where one lives out her life in its entirety, ALONE; fighting battles, some won, some lost, real or imagined, to her benefit or detriment.

Chapter one discussed polarity or the fact that with everything that exists there is an opposite. Chapter one further discussed the need to avoid extremes; for to lean too far towards one extreme would result in the neglect of the opposite (extreme). Man's preoccupation with his external world has caused him to neglect his not so obvious mental world. Think about this for a moment: if most or all that is your external life is the result of your internal life/mind/thoughts, then understandably a life that neglects the mind is a life of disappointment and disaster. For the person who neglects the mind; or for those who cause damaged to the brain due to the bad habits of smoking, drinking, etc., it must be realize that though appearing to be separate, these polar opposites (mind & external life) are part and parcel, meaning ONE. The same applies to the builder of "air castles"; or persons who dreams much, but builds or produces very little (externally). All of his time is spent in his mind, imagining accomplishments; accomplishments which he never physically attempts to achieve. Ultimately, the neglect of either one will result in the destruction of the other. As

I stated earlier, home is an interesting concept. People reside in the shadows, but believe otherwise; and it is their preoccupation with the "otherwise", that results in an inability to recognize the need for light (learning) amidst the shadows.

My intent in this chapter is to demonstrate the reality that though a man's life appears to play itself out in the third dimension (physical world), his outward behavior is a mere dramatization of what he thinks. Everyday there are persons who struggle to establish themselves or find their place in the scheme of things, but fail to make <u>any investment</u> at all into their mental life (any potentially progressive investments that is). Instead what's collected in the mind of the individual is all of the junk; the worry, stress and similar poisons which further inhibit the individual's potential for progress;

ultimately causing one's life to *seem* disappointing and unfulfilled; even unbearable. To me, information is money; for the more you know (in this society) the more valuable you are. Every new idea, every new thing learned has an undeterminable value. Imagine that you invested as much time and energy into your thinking, as you do your finances and other possessions; how well off would you be?

Part three

TIME TRAVEL

In the next two chapters I am going to discuss what I realized to be two of the greatest hindrances of man. His first hindrance is his past.

Time and again each of us as human beings spend moments of our life dissatisfied. For some, the time spent dissatisfied is only for a moment; but for others, dissatisfaction is felt without end. Feelings of dissatisfaction and disappointment are, in many cases, the result of regret felt for choices made in our past. Regularly, a woman beats herself up for exhibiting an unproductive behavior or for choosing an action that failed to produce an outcome she desired. So many of us are plagued with feelings of disappointment and dissatisfaction for the very same reasons; and so our inability to let go of yesterday or our dissatisfaction with choices made yesterday becomes one of our greatest obstacles.

A man reflects on a disruption in his personal relationship that had taken place a year into his past. Amazingly, he travels back into time (memory) and re-experiences the pain and disappointment relative to that moment; so much so, that he actually **re-invokes** former feelings associated with the past experience into his present experience. As a result, said (past) experience is <u>relived</u> all over again as if it had 'just happened' in the (present) moment. The above mentioned feet are performed by so many every single day. Who says that a man can't time travel?

Unfortunately, for whatever reason human beings struggle with the idea that there are no do-overs; that whatever has happened yesterday, has passed into oblivion; and our preoccupation with moments in our past inhibits our ability to move forward. Take for example the idea of a man who is unemployed and who is searching for employment opportunities. In his immediate past the quest for employment bore no fruit; naturally he grew dissatisfied, because of his lack of success. As the days go by the search for employment appears bleak; his self-confidence diminishes and eventually, he stops looking. After about a week of relaxation he decides to give it another go; only this time after getting dressed and collecting his resume, he gets to the door, but never exits. Unfortunately his thoughts about his past failures made him apprehensive about going out and asking for work. He began to think "why even bother, I'm not going to get hired anyway". Ultimately, his confronting his circumstances with apprehension, caused by his fear of failing resulted in the evitable. Being afraid of failure led him to avoid the opportunity to fail by not applying for the job in the first place; which in the end became his failure after all. In this instance, he is experiencing the disappointment of rejection by his own hand. "He" rejected himself, in order to avoid experiencing rejection that he assumed and feared was coming from someone else, whom he has never even had the pleasure of meeting.

A woman meets a man and becomes very excited about the potential of a new relationship. He is intelligent, attractive, industrious, and possesses so many other qualities that a woman desires in a potential mate. Though this new guy has all of these great qualities to his credit, the woman never allows herself to totally commit; she has experienced so much disappointment in her past personal relationships, that she is terrified of reliving similar circumstances. This fear of disappointment in love causes her to approach her new potential relationship with apprehension. What she does not know is that this new guy senses her apprehension and in turn becomes apprehensive himself. Ladies and gentlemen this is the classic failure of a relationship. By her being apprehensive, her new boyfriend who recognizes her apprehension becomes apprehensive and a wedge is established between the two. Ultimately, the relationship is doomed from the start and what was most feared by the woman is assured (another failed relationship). If my preoccupation with the infidelity of my past mate(s) causes me to not trust the sincerity of present or future mates, I will never allow myself the opportunity to experience a truly fulfilling relationship for fear that it will fail. My behavior would do no more than teleport past feelings associated with past circumstances into the present. If for every step a man took forward he followed that forward step with two steps backwards, where would he end up? Disappointment due to a lack of progress is assured.

It is unfortunate that so many of us struggle with our pasts decisions and / or experiences; but what must be understood is that forward movement will continue to be a struggle for as long as we expend countless energy traveling into yesterday. No person on this planet can travel due North with absolute accuracy, while facing (and in most cases, traveling) due south. If the message in part one of this book clarified nothing else, it made clear that too much focus to one extreme (i.e. the past) causes the neglect and eventual destruction of the opposite extreme.

Part Four

THERE IS NO TOMORROW

The previous chapter discussed one of the two greatest hindrances to man; that being his preoccupation with his past. Man's other greatest hindrance is his preoccupation with his future.

I know that reading the above statement will cause many to disagree with the idea of one's preoccupation with tomorrow hindering his progress. I only asked that before allowing your mind to shut off or before disagreeing, you at least give due consideration to what I am about to say.

While the idea of one's past hindering his progress might be easily understood, the idea that one's concern about his future might create for him a fate similar to the aforementioned understandably is puzzling to some; but many of us experience a great amount of fear and stress when contemplating our future. In fact, if you compile the uncertainty of tomorrow with our constant struggles to make definite decisions, my reasoning might become clearer. Think about some of the examples mentioned in the previous chapter. The man who experienced failure in his previous attempts to find an occupation gave up in the end, due to the <u>assumption</u> (prediction) that he would not succeed at finding a job. His choice to no longer look for a job was based on his expected failure (future tense). His fears associated with a potential _future outcome_ caused him to not make an effort in the moment. This brings us to the position that I am presenting to you: one of the greatest causes of disappointment and, which ultimately leads to failure is <u>expectation</u>, or more particularly, hope absent effort. Either a person assumes the worse as with the unemployed gentlemen, or something that one might have been expecting does not come into fruition. In both cases the individual(s) concerned will usually feel disappointed and / or dissatisfied with the outcome(s). These persons tend to feel defeated, which leads to feelings of inadequacy, self doubt, and ultimately their own undoing.

Naturally you might be thinking "well, what do we do, not plan for our future?" No, that is not what I am saying. What comes under question is <u>the amount of</u> <u>value you place on the thing expected</u>. If you are a person who validates yourself by the things you possess, by the people with whom you associate, or by your "accomplishments", then your dissatisfaction is understood. Should one or more of these things not pan out, the person in question begins to question their significance and their value. On the contrary, if you do not place value on your possessions, your associates, your accomplishments, etc., losing any of these things will have very little (negative) effect on you. (Read my book, the Key to Character for a further discussion of personal significance) People are so afraid of tomorrow's disappointment that they walk, speak, and even breathe with apprehension. Consider the woman mentioned in the previous chapter; she had experienced so much disappointment in her past personal relationships, that she never allowed herself to commit herself 100% in her new relationship, for fear of experiencing a similar disappointment. As you can see many of us even fear the expected (future) loss, disappointment, ridicule, embarrassment, etc., associated with our past experiences. This idea reminds me of a quote that I often make: "many of us spend so much of our time and energy trying not to die, that we forget to live." People, I assure you that a life lived with apprehension is not a life at all.

All of us have been taught ideas of what constitutes wins and losses. Our desire(s) to win, coupled with our desire(s) to avoid loss are a major cause of the stress experienced by each of us daily. Not knowing what tomorrow has in store for us drives us to indulge in activities (alcohol, drugs, promiscuity, etc.) or to exhibit behavior (especially frustration and vulnerability) that assures no more than our absolute destruction. As mentioned in an earlier chapter, there are no do-overs. Yesterday is gone and you cannot get it back. What's done is done; let it rest. You would do yourself a great service by simply realizing the value or lesson associated with the past experience, improving your behavior/choices/etc., and not repeating such undesirable circumstances as you continue to live your life. What you must also understand is that there is in fact <u>no</u> tomorrow. Think about it; when you arrive to tomorrow, it'll be today. When you arrive to next week, it'll be this week; and the next minute, this minute; next year will be this year. The truth is, you never 'really' reach or even witness a tomorrow. "Tomorrow" is a concept at best that attempts to capture the idea of "a distance or a point in space/time", which is essentially no different, nor any less local than where you are currently sitting or standing right now. Here's a test: remain where you are right now for 24 hours; outside of increasing muscle fatigue and hunger pains, or the Earth spinning on its axis, causing the Sun to appear to disappear, make a note of what about "the day itself" actually changes (specifically to a "tomorrow"). Better yet, just explain to anyone what constitutes tomorrow. Good luck.

How is it that we have become so illusioned that we live in fear of an idea that never materializes? Our fears of not achieving our goals, dreams, wishes, etc, inhibits us all in every way imaginable. This tendency to self-destruct has become a common behavior of us all. Do I need to reiterate the clinical definition of insanity? Maybe so.

The clinical definition of insanity is to do the same thing over and over again, each time expecting a different result.

Throughout the entirety of each and every one of our lives, we have made plans repeatedly. Very, very seldom has ANY of our plans EVER turned out exactly the way that we had envisioned. Nevertheless, each and every one of us acts shocked and is devastated when our efforts fail to produce the desired outcome. So, we continue to plan, fail, and stress. How insane are you?

At what point do we realize that we need to plan with elasticity; to not be attached to any particular desired outcome, but instead appreciate the outcomes that we do experience? Knowing that very little has ever turned out exactly the way you've expected, why would you expect your next plan to produce at any greater level of accuracy? I am not saying that prediction is impossible; only that most of us aren't any good at predicting outcomes. This scenario reveals one uncomfortable truth: that your disappointment and unfortunate undoing is self-inflicted.

Part Five

NOW

"In a right angled triangle: the square of the hypotenuse is equal to the sum of the squares of the other two sides."

- Pythagorean Theorem

You might ask: "What was the purpose of this Author's proof of extremes; particularly yesterday and tomorrow?"

My intent is to prove to the reader one ever escaping (hidden) reality; that the key to solving the riddle of extremes resides in the middle.

Our preoccupations with yesterday and tomorrow causes each of us to neglect the most important and best part, TODAY.

Our continual departure from the NOW into shadow time (past/future) leaves absolutely little to no focus on the moment, resulting in stagnation; for it is in the NOW, via of our choices and actions that we simultaneously lay out our history, which in turn become our foundation for the future. If there is no decision and no action in the NOW, there will be no traces of yesterday and so no ground work performed to assure our tomorrow.

There are many areas of our life where the principle of equilibrium is demonstrated; where the middle road has proven to be the best path. For example: the sum total and so the best part of a Man and a Woman is the offspring. Communication sets in the "middle ground" between opposite-equals. When communication fails, imbalance (polarity) is the result. Love, dwelling in the center of a Man and a Woman in a relationship is the connection or the tie that binds; for absent the principle of love, all is in disarray. The "hand-shake" too lies in the middle of two people symbolizing a compromise or shared vision; a common ground. The conscious mind lies in the in-between of internal and external life; so understandably to be unaware in the moment is to deny one the opportunity to invest in him/herself.

There are countless examples of the need for balance and equilibrium between opposites; two of the most obvious examples of extremes being war and peace; where understanding and tolerance is the solution.

Spend a minute contemplating the moment. Try your best not to think about what happened in each second that has already past. Do not think about yesterday, and do not think about what you have to do in the next hour; just stay HERE. Remain attentive to ever word you read without allowing your mind to wander. Stay with me; only 30 more seconds remaining; there is nothing else to consider except these words that you are reading right NOW. NOW; see, that is the idea; to stay in the NOW. Ok, stop and answer this: while focusing on the above message, did anything else come to mind? Did you feel any stress or worry? Did you feel anything at all? If you were able to remain in the moment, you would not have experienced any of the above feelings. Feelings of worry, stress, dissatisfaction, etc, are directly related to (negative) thoughts about our past and future. A better control over *"where we place our **attention**"* will relieve us of so many of the negative emotions we are accustomed to experiencing. Practice the above test enough, and I assure you that it will become second nature.

The ideas expressed in this small book will prove to be invaluable to the person(s) seeking to change their lives. It is the **choices** we make that help to shape our circumstances. If we want different circumstances, we have to begin to *choose differently*. While the contrast or contradictions or polarity described in this book creates, for each and every one of us, challenges; such challenges or conflict(s) are the sculptors' tools used to carve out the intricacies of one's thinking, one's appearance and the differing details of one's life. These conflicts provide the controversy, losses, confusion and triumphs that serve as those very necessary lessons that are critical to our development as Human Beings. These spaces or extremes of loss and victory are not where we are to remain; but it is instead in the in-between or the compromise of these extremes where we will find the equilibrium and balance or the peace and harmony that we so desperately need. There is nobody home, but you; you and you alone have to power to improve your circumstances, and so, your life. All you have to do is realize this:

"In order to change your world, all you have to do is change your mind."

NOW

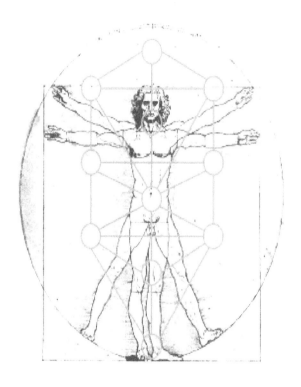

About the Author

Khalid El Bey

Khalid El Bey attended Virginia State University in Petersburg, Virginia as a Social Work Major, and studied Psychology at Empire State College in Saratoga Springs, New York. He has conducted independent research in history and law, and has studied non-traditional subjects, such as Astrology, Numerology and Qabala to name a few. He is the co-founder of the Creative Research Society, whose main focus is the re-education of the so-called African American and he is also an active member of the Ancient and Primitive Rite of Memphis & Misraim (freemasonry).

Mr. Bey has lectured at numerous events on the campuses of colleges and universities, as well as at a number of community events along the East coast and in the Midwest and has spoken extensively about the questionable origins of man, mans personal identity and human relationships. Mr. Bey is also very active in a number of community organizations in Syracuse, New York, where he's located. Currently Mr. Bey is serving his first term as a City Councilor in the City of Syracuse (New York).

An insightful man, his favorite quote is: "In order to change the world, all one has to do is change his mind."

Made in the USA
Middletown, DE
18 December 2022